HONG KONG: GROWING PAINS

Jon Ng

Proverse Hong Kong

November 2020

HONG KONG: GROWING PAINS is an exploration of the city of Hong Kong, detailing experiences that exist within its ever-changing space, examining some of the pressures felt while growing up in the financial entrepôt, before moving on to the translation of emotions felt during the tumultuous second half of 2019, as protests rocked the amorphous Special Administrative Region. *Hong Kong: Growing Pains* is Jon Ng's first published collection.

JON NG lives in Hong Kong, where he writes poetry and teaches English literature. He was born and raised in Canada. His subsequent move to Hong Kong has left him pondering his own identity as a non-Cantonese speaker in this people and culture-dense city. His work has appeared in a few publications, winning second runner-up in 2019 for *Hong Kong's Top Story* Competition, on the online platform of *EastLit* in 2015 and in the poetry anthology *Twin Cities* in 2018.

HONG KONG GROWING PAINS

Jon Ng

Proverse Hong Kong

Hong Kong Growing Pains
By Jon Ng
Alternate first edition published in paperback in Hong Kong
by Proverse Hong Kong, November 2020.
ISBN-13: 978-988-8492-12-1
First edition published in paperback in Hong Kong
by Proverse Hong Kong, November 2020.
ISBN-13: 978-988-8492-13-8

Enquiries to Proverse Hong Kong
P.O. Box 259, Tung Chung Post Office,
Lantau, NT, Hong Kong SAR, China.
Email: proverse@netvigator.com;
Web: www.proversepublishing.com

Author photo by Jon Ng
Cover design by Aceler Chua

British Library Cataloguing in Publication Data
A catalogue record for the first paperback edition
is available from the British Library

Prior Publication Acknowledgements

An earlier version of, 'Morning Music', was originally published in the March 2013 edition of the online journal *EastLit*. A huge acknowledgement, with love and thanks, is due to Michael Liaw, Proverse Publishing for their patience and guidance, and Aceler Chua for designing and putting together the cover art.

For the Nandas,
Michael,
My wife,
And all those
Who helped me stand
And taught me what to stand for

HONG KONG: GROWING PAINS

JON NG

HERITAGE

Heritage

Did you know?
I once wrote a few lines to a professor-poet
querying if she thought that the stigma of having an Asian
name
would restrict me to writing about simply Asian things.

She told me, in kinder words than these,
to *open my eyes*.
She said that if I saw that I had nothing to write about
then perhaps I wasn't looking at the scenes
that've shaped my life.

I never replied out of shame
and out of respect for my burning face.
Yet it turns out now that in every line I place
a little bit of my heritage
courage
and I sign them off with my Asian name.

Dinnertime Shambles

The sounds of china clinking
perfect plate upon plate
jolts me back to wakefulness
as I agitate my fingertips against the tablecloth
waiting for dinner to begin, to be served.

For one who has always walked free,
eating burgers as he talked,
seeing meals as breaks between classes,
school, sleep and now jobs,
silverware placements are glimmering,
shimmering manacles;
tabletop conversations are interrogations,
pouring tea is part of a duty
and clearing plates is to sate
not my appetite but the eyes
of those who have come before me,
and know the value of no waste.

I am a terror here, an aberration –
uncouth, uncivilized, from some barbaric nation;
the games begin with musical chairs
as people stand and shuffle to greet
relatives long lost or cousins older than they,
juggling dozens of names with numbers and in order,
while myself, I shuffle shyly into handshakes.

After rotating seats about three times
my eyes slouch over to tea,
two kettles the same, one clean water
the other stained inside, both equally
my responsibility. At the same time,
My hands clink with forks and knives

while others use sticks, and I try —
but they slip and my face burns
as kindly I'm reminded that
that spoon is for soup, dear,
and that small one's for dessert;
can we have forks and knives
for this one over here?

I've gotten better now.
Sticks have become second hands and
All dinners end with signatures on bills and farewells.
I know the meal serving routines
Where elders come first and then the youngest
and I've learnt how some lies of
we'll help ourselves are
"We expect you to"
All confused with sometimes
"We really do
help ourselves to our own food."

Watch tea levels.
Don't take too much.
Don't take the last portion.
Now you can take it.
Finish up the plate.
Dumb.
That part of the duck was
her grandma's favorite.

Soup Noodles

The wisdom goes as follows:
The longer you take to sip your soup
And eat your noodles – the more the two suffuse
In a thickening of what was once thin,
In a phenomenon of soup levels dropping to a drought,
A vanishing of the broth you were promised,
All because you *took your time.*

On the corner of a street that has undergone
Costume change after costume change
Survives my noodle store, *Tsim Tsai Kee*, which was once
Filled with round tables speckled white and blue,
Cold and smooth, matching the china and the sky
That all the world used to be served in.
We slurped 10 dollars of deliciousness down
Every Sunday after a different sort of school,
Back when God was taught as an eternal sort of thing.

In just under two decades
The tenner has swelled to twenty and change,
While the shrimp wonton has shrunk and
The decor has been blazed down from family round spaces
To dark mahogany that keep the business-people
Coming, going, chewing, slurping, churning people
So what's eaten inside, is paid for outside,
And workers are sent back office-side.

When later, elsewhere, I remark on this change,
My companions act as if I am deranged,
As if the knowledge of materialism and inflation
Were sufficient enough to explain it all away.

What those economists don't realize
Is my comment was not one of complaint,
Merely vocalization of how I don't mind the decor change,
Or the fattening of the prices, for I still return all the same,
As the compassionate faces that serve my bowls in
       thickening skin
And darkening ridges greet me the same way
– *wei, lang zai* – over two decades.

When those faces fade
It won't matter if they serve their noodles to me
On their Michelin Awards as plates:

Whatever thin string they serve me,
And whatever reservoir of soup,
I'll see the dish thick as rope,
The soup dry as bone,
And from that day on,
I will always leave hungry.

---

wei, lang zai: a common Cantonese greeting: "Hey, handsome boy".

Computography

Characters, each one a finger wide,
finger high. Placed like mahjong tiles
seemingly neatly shuffled but out of place,
just enough so that they're not terracotta
soldiers, but each, one button with blank eyes.

Each character is a piece of a word that has
sounds, so that's why Ga Gheen likes to be
called Ah-Fa. Ah-Fa shows me how to make
his English name, just like how he shows me which
squares makes which stroke in which direction.
Work is so much faster on the computer, he
sometimes says to his parents. I don't agree.

I used to do calligraphy. The slimness and flow
of the words was wonder. It was movement.
River flow, dots of water, falling, splashed. Fire
when sounded *"Fwor"*, bit the roof of your mouth.
On page I licked it into man size canvases
with the tip of the brush's tongue. Let it sizzle
at its edges. Now, on the computer, everything
looks the same. I sluice meaning through by fingers,
my daughter jabs them into the computer. Sometimes
I try. Just when I think I'm getting the hang of it,
neck craned forward, they turn off the screen.
Bad for my eyes. I shuffle off. As they please.

They've given me a place where I can check for mail,
But I don't even pretend that I use it anymore.
So they show me how to see their pictures, this button,
for photos of England with themselves in them.
Spain. Good music, and dancing. Beautiful women.

They've showed me emails, and I've asked them to
read them out loud. Sometimes they say they're junk.
Nobody tells me why. I don't see why they're junk.

My granddaughter's daughter sits on my thigh.
She writes away. Are those strokes I eye? No.
Characters on her phone. Child's finger size.

Bus Rides

The man gazes, enraptured
By the girls singing on the screen.
Immersion is full, complete.
Earphones, HD.

I wonder what he is captured by,
The flesh, the fantasy, the music,
The cinematography? He taps out
To a library of videos, each one an MV.

The bus we are on is taking us
Somewhere, bound by highway
And lines, and holds in its travel time
At least two voyeurs, transfixed by what they see.

HD: High-Definition
MV: Music Video

Discontent

Sterile white walls, riverhum of
fluorescent lights and array of desks
in a Stonehenge. An unfettered
natural office state.

Lifts lift-off from years
of engineering. They arrive with
a ding and a carriage full
of people with eyes uncaring.

Estranged labor. Education
has taught enough to recognise it,
and dissatisfaction murmurs below cheekbones
like the low growl of thunder
underneath heavy brows
and eyes clouded over.

Still, for all of the discontent
and realization, time flows and
pushes away at water-wheels;
and production rises and sets,
days always ending with dusk
pushing to the end of the month
so that numbers will grow
and the future will not have sunk.

Skin, hopes and bones
skitter out as husks
tap out time cards,
each increment
investing, not in enlightenment,
but in courage enough
to one day, not show up.

Rain

Even on sunny days we can write of rain,
Because the sun has taken away only for a while
Those buoyant puddles that try to keep our feet up
As solidly as the earth, but are met with curses as, instead,
Faith is rewarded with embracing ankle slaps of wet.

It's the monotony of soft beats that's missing on summer
days,
Because the rain bleaches, though we don't know it.
So used are we to bleach making sweet, sweet white,
But the rain is not snow, sugar, or pure; it is static,
White-and-grey and the clattering
Sound of constant platter on windows.
But if we listen closely – individually,
What they'll be is soft plinking on concrete,
The upper end of piano keys.

Almost in harmony:
Rain makes umbrellas come out with uniform whumps,
Hydraulic pumps popping out as regularly as the peering
Of fleshy faces with irises pointed up in fear of being caught
Out wet, staining white and black suits: penguins outside of
igloos.
Rain makes wheels suddenly into potential cold-volcano
burps
And spinning sprays like the slaps of a whale's tail against the
sea
And though each raindrop is a kamikaze
Plummeting from the haze we once worshipped as heaven:
Wet stains and cold clasps only bring wishes
To soon be dry again.

How I wish we played in the rain again,
Because in the rain we've all learned
To curse, react about the same.
We'll never see it, only take umbrage
From hanging umbrella spokes
And the jostling for dry places —
But on rainy days, we are all connected
In a wonderful, thankless thought of:
God, how I hate the rain.

Morning Music

Falling shower water rushes down plastic pipes
Like cybernetic sounds from a distant future;
Not rumbling like present-day hulking cargo trains
But like garbled data these waterfalls shred
As warbling ukuleles can, playing in the morning song
Of dirty apartment blocks in Hong Kong.

Slamming doors and table screeches act next
As the bass section of this jazz band, and for rhythm,
Lifts scrape the walls as they rise and descend
Grunting like blunted fingernails across washboards.
Meanwhile upstairs footsteps begin the shuffle beat
(door) slam, step and step, step and step, step and step.

Then the mothers scream at children who bawl,
Construction workers swear for the sake of it.
Vocalists resonate through windows that meet
In central, sunless spires full of putrid air.
Our vocalists' amplifiers are ceramic, tiled hallways,
Alarms sound, cabinets shut, lifts shudder up and down.

The set usually reaches its peak then around ten.
Silence. The riffing's vanished, the climax reached.
Nobody wakes up another and no new instrument
Is needed – everyone's awake, off to another day.
At night the children return before seven, some adults past
ten.
No uniformity then, no music to play them in.

But come the next morning, there will come another song.

Solitude on a Balcony

the fog of the harbour drifts lazily, listlessly.

the sun contorts my face into narrow lines
into squints
a scrunched nose
a crossed forehead and thin cheek lines.

the glint of our star coming from far above
is vacuumed into the sea far below
gathered into shimmering water-tethered confetti pieces,
till rusty hulls scatter them into stripes.
the sea is a golden zebra in some places,
in most others, undulating bands of a blue superhero's skin.

meanwhile, a helicopter thrums by at eye level.
a pair of kites shriek from their urban perches.
they leap off but for birds, gravity's in reverse –
thermals send them spiralling into slow circles
up – down – neither – suspended – till they sparkle into
brown specks.

eventually I am called from my space
as a glass door shudders open.
an unopened pack of cigarettes
is grabbed by another's hand.
a flick beside my ear: tiny heat, tender.

as the butt begins its birth, the sun sets.

Tai Koo Promenade

As time passes, I will continue to claim,
As I have always said, that walking down
The paths between the residential community,
The bay, and another series of towers, spires,
At night-time you are inspired by stars,
Stars, stars, but not by those in the sky,
But the lights that speckle across the sea,
In constellations of apartments where each
Each light serves as a solar system,
Each light a star where inside, a family resides.

As the lights wink, I shrink, and I feel as all those
Must, as the universe unfolds before me in reminder
That I am just another speck of dust, and yet even
As I watch, as I scribe, I am reminded, re-reading
These lines, that despite my size, for a moment,
This infinitesimal verse? It maintains a universe.

Lan Kwai Nights

Prowling the emptying streets;
the pavement seems slicker than normal,
sweating from between the cracks
of orange bricked sidewalks.

Yet somehow the air feels parched.

The stumble is the rhythm of the walks,
accented by slurred tongues and blaring pop songs.
another drink, sir? *No – I've had enough –*
lips reply – delayed – between shisha puffs.

Some eyes boggle as they pay the bills,
others just slap cards into tomorrow.
A boy hoots like an owl from his perch
on the sidewalk and a girl laughs. Maniacs.

Neon lights hide the night.
The melting into daybreak echoes in the sky.
Tomorrow work comes early but it's too late
To sleep early now – Empty boasts.
A toast from across the street.
Taxi home. Vomit somewhere.
The driver swears.

Wake to the payment of a fare.

"Shisha": also known as "hookah", for smoking flavoured tobacco.

City Seats

Like movie theatres, seating pre-arranged
But your screen the views of hills and sea:
The fates parted the landscape for you
Like curtains, for on slopes they paved you roads
And leveled flat the shoulders of mountains
Where once, trees did not need to search
For their own natural perch for constant growth:
But man cut down for you those ancients
To make on high for you those cement domes
And you paid – paid with fortunes for the space
That entire family trees could never make.

Down below, front rows, the people watch
The same city unfold in clusters;
Necks craned in beds the size of two coffins,
Three people wide, feet touching their roofs
Cage homes – three wide, six deep,
Six feet stacked in lightless, dreamless sleep,
Paying in rent for bunk beds so they can
Dump rest into tomorrow, cradling children
On rusted foldable tables that serve for dinner,
Study, gambling leisure, for elbows attached
To thin arms and gazes diluted by blank eyes.

Your thrones sit above valleys
Curves like supple fat on the sides of bodies
While the rest of us sit in thin sticks
Of apartments with their spines the lifts
That rumble sounds and colour in duotone,
Rhythms of life dressed in penguin costumes,
Old films with cackling sounds of opportunity
That groan as they creak open, and croak
As we wait for promotions, and resign ourselves
To the moment that promises are broken;

You watch racecourses from your homes
Far enough away so that you can see us run,
Marathons for us, you, watching our lines,
Graphs, gambling on winners and losers
Though the winning and losing's already done.

If I could make a wish that would be laid on everyone,
It would be to count our blessings, one by one,
Dollar by dollar, each second without falter
Until the census of blessings is tallied to a sum.
While you'd still be counting, it'd at least give
A couple hundred years of a chance for us
To catch up to you who'd won, won,
Living in victory, before you'd even begun.

GROWING PAINS

Growing Pains

Eyes are always about the same size,
Two attentive spotlights –
Yet children's eyes are never thought the same
Since they stand at lower heights.

But if they see as much as we do,
Then how could we forget,
These children, candles burning bright
As innocence melts away,
Sculpt themselves into
Their flaky, waxen selves. –
But what adults show and tell
Can snuff their dreams out,
Can make their whole world, Hell.

The Wet Market

You do not understand. You take my hand
and you lead me meandering over a soaked,
tiled floor, scowling, pulling harder and then yanking.

It has been scrubbed over. Washed, sprayed. It is too bright.
I've seen the cleaners at night. The entrance is too wide.
It gapes at me. There is sunlight on the other side.

You turn and, framing your gritted teeth,
you use your public, mother's voice. You implore
me to pick up my pace. You remove my schoolbag.

You do not see it. The clouds that hover here,
the red of dismemberment at the butchers,
the yellow rot crawling all over the vegetable stands,

the black mist seemingly visible only to me
and the eyelidless fish, their tails flapping away
on beds of white ice, the floor leaking bright red.

It has been scrubbed over. Ceramic does not
swallow. The floor tastes different from blood.
But the stench tells a different story. You do not smell it.

Beyond the market is a sunflower coloured bus.
It is filled with little fingers like mine, little faces,
little feet. You demand a kiss from me for your cheek.

I am not the last to arrive. I try to point that out
but you're already gone. They went the long way around.
In the sun, not through the shade. Arriving on time.

The bus driver asks me again how I am this morning.
Like every other day I reply the same way. "I just can't
breathe."
Whether or not he hears me, the door closes. We stick to
routine.

Mother Calls

When I was a child my mother used to console us with
At least when I die God will tell me
that in his eyes I have done all that was right
in order to raise you children in His name.
She was very much into self-sacrifice.

But some other things that she told us were
that her actions, though they never showed love,
meant love, and though her words and lullabies
were never pleasant, she explained that they gave her
pleasure;
and so, as sons are connected to the mother,
we were to feel pleasure from her words, exactly as they were
spoken.

Years later, she still calls to ask which task
I've put myself to work at. Of course, I must explain
I am teeming with success and joy, for which she'll pat her
back
and praise the Lord, but not before she asks
What my monthly salary's at, and how I mean to double that.

Before the phone call ends,
She asks, morning, night, in the afternoon:
"Are you going to visit soon?"

I don't say no. But if I say that I want time
To write instead, she'll insist, in a fib, she has the space
– And alongside – the supposed peace and quiet.
So I say I have to work, earn a salary that inflates her pride.
Then a click. On my side, a swipe, my heart heavy
With years of unheard goodbyes.

Arcade Games

We dropped our tokens into machines,
Our feet sticky on the spilt-soda floor,
And our eyes snapped at the excitement of
All the flashing lights and round joysticks
And buttons to smash,
Kinetic energy made electric made
Into numbers made into graphics made to react.

And as the coins jangled down through
The stoic lips of the machines, and rattled
Into the guts of those hulking, cliff-shaped beasts,
Our bodies too demanded responses
As, high on the hormones of competition,
We mashed our way through match after match,
Egos inflating, deflating, based on practice
And the resulting widths of neuroplastic paths,
Paving the way for sparks shot through from synapse
To synapse until the answers to our efforts appeared,
And a winner and loser was made clear.

Player One. Player Two.
You win. You lose.

Where we went after school
We learned to fish, to ride,
To drive where we were told to,
To fight because we were supposed to,
To shoot at the enemies or for the stars that
They chose for you, to dance to the neon arrows
In the direction and ways you were scored to.

Time out. KO. No prize for you.
Continue?

We had our matches and our runs,
We dropped our hours one by one,
We played the games we learned to play,
But learnt far too late
(Or never for long enough anyway)
That day after day, the moment we paid to play:

Win or Lose?
Buying in was
Predestined resignation
Of the right to choose.

A city park and football pitch

How are little children's footfalls so much louder
than their full-sized adult counterparts?
They blaze like little fireworks if you watch the
concrete pitch as you might at night.

The soles clap about with brand-name yellows,
Tick-mark orange-reds and as they wobble around,
They sound out with explosions of laughter
As their voices call for the ball, and fouls.

Yet, true to this city's landscape,
not twenty metres off, buses roar by, and
branching roads break off; highways rise.

Pigmentations of grey solidify in the sky,
and beneath those fluorescent clothes, the grey
Grows in the lungs of children kicking high.

The lady in charge screams at young girls riding bikes
crossing the sanctity of the place, her voice hoarse
but not with concern for their safety from flying balls,
but because it is her right; she's booked the space after all.

After she's shouted herself all red, she returns to the side
and counts with her coach the number of children who run,
and with green eyes multiplies and pockets the sum.
While the children score, she calls absentees, and the goals are
more than one.

Shadows of our Siblings

I've always been overshadowed
By thinking it to be fact,
That my brothers were smarter than me.

They tested us all at separate stages
For giftedness, and out of the three
I was the black sheep.

So while I coloured between lines,
They did geometry,
And when I finally learnt shapes
And thought I'd caught up,
They began work in 3D.

Physics they called it,
The way the world worked.
And their equations – to my shock – never had
The dot line dot division symbol after studying *that*.

Throughout all of those years
I never acknowledged that I was the youngest
By two years and four years respectively,
And though, to suggest zero, two and four
Made no difference arithmetically was absurd,
I bought it without protest;
I suppose that's why I'm the dullest.

Library Warriors

Central Library. Exam Period.

No matter the uniform, the action's the same:
Library opening hour: they surge up the plane
To the desks they hunker down, bunkered, equipment gathered,
Bags set; notes reloaded to the proper subject matter.

They arrange themselves in the seats that remain
Clocks tick on pace with flips of pages, no refrain,
The sun dashes its way across the sky
Doors close, end the skirmish unseen by the eye.

They depart in droves, notebooks in hand
Pens sheathed in their holsters, papers scarred across the skin.
To their homes they retreat but on their books their minds linger,
Fighting for the glory of that eternal, parental, crucial "A" hunger.

The Textbook is a Liar

The textbook is a liar
not because its edges are cut clean,
or the way its pages lie shimmering
glossy like the preening lips
of women on TV;

I've no problem with the content
or the jargon explained in neat glossaries
at the end of every chapter,
I've no issue with the weight either
or with the pages straining to tear away
from the spine that binds them together,
I've not even a problem with the illustrations
for even though its depicted it that way,
I've learnt by now
that the vagina doesn't look exactly like that;

But:

The textbook is a liar because after finishing it
I'm supposed to suppose I've become smarter,
yet even without the recommendations
from authors pushing books to read further,
whenever I close those monstrosities
all I feel is dumb – minute – petite – microscopic,
and I curl right back up and dream of simpler days
when knowing nothing felt like knowing everything,
and that felt fine, no matter how wrong that was.

Model Roles

Yellow ribbons and young hearts,
Carrying Corporate ID cards.

Wear a suit or
sit amongst soot
equally ignored
as long at least
begging looks busy.

"Worthless employee",
"Bottom of the hierarchy" –
The uniforms around defining
Security, janitor, cook.

It's the ideal look.
Slim waist, strong arms,
good grades, a graduation cap
to keep you warm.

How to be
a Primary One child:
Learn Two
instruments
Know Three
languages
Before Four
years old.
Nine years later,
Ten A stars
else that's all we wrote.

Syllabus:
Learn the colors.
Taxi-red to
Take me where
I want to go.
Brown is good.
Five-hundred dollar note.

Now learn the maths.
The higher the better.
Figures are better
than learning about books.

Geography time.
You can travel once you're rich.
History time.
No one remembers the poor
Except to remember that
Not being this, is what education's for.

For extra-curriculars
Since your parents are never home
Go have an extra class.
Just be glad you're not the class teacher
when your grades come back.

Yellow ribbon, young hearts.
Crushed to Corporate ID Cards.

Two Students: S.C. and T.

S.C.

Erised – she called it –
A reflection from the world of wizardry –
I found it, saw into it –
It's here – what does it reflect?

You don't see my parents in
A silhouette about me?
Don't hear it? What do I want?
Let me ask Erised. Uh-huh.
Right. What do I want?
What they said.

T.

It seems *so fun* on the outer edge of the gyre,
On the extremities of something, spinning
At breakneck speeds for better or worse.

I have been in the middle for so long
That even I am beginning to forget myself.
That I am slow does not need to be told
To me. Others by the time they snap away
From the centre whip off at breakneck speeds.

By the time it is my time to leave from the middle
I will still be here. They will look at me in the future
Wondering how it is that I've gone nowhere.

I am neither good, nor bad. I am the centre
Of morality, and I will never be on the silver
Screen. I have never needed hopes or dreams,
And I remind you, value, is something *you* placed on *me*.

"Erised": a reference to "The Mirror of Erised" in J.K. Rowling's
Harry Potter and the Philosopher's Stone, "Erised" is the name of a
mirror that reflects one's inner desires. ("Erised" is "desire" spelt
backwards.)

Where Growing Goes

1.

For a fifth of your life,
We've dripped knowledge
About the world,
Letting ideas drizzle like
A springtime rain,
Light, timid, non-committal.

And at schools, as gardens
Were tender and tended to,
Attendance was a delight as,
Though you needed no prescription,
Knowledge brought on knowledge
Like buds on tangled vines,
And language blossomed *knowing,*
While your teachers marvelled
About Wittgenstein.

Limits were fiction then,
And the wind was a cooling fan
Which could relieve, or
Retrieve the imagination to whisk it
To the touchless realms,
Where answers were friendly spectres,
And the world, an infinite playpen, then –

2.

Then?
Knowledge gained weight,
And fell as if rain and mist
Were one and the same,
And though books were books

The mist seemed like it ate
Through covers and pages
Permeating learning, morphing it
From pleasure to a necessary hate.

See, the clouds swelled and stained
From the light white of those days,
From bleating wool to pelt of grey,
And falling one after another like comrades,
Caught by the links that we as humans had made,
We dragged down Time, and shaped it,
Valued it by its shrinking proximity
To application dates for Universities
And gave those Places crowns
While Time and Knowledge were run aground.

3.

I wish I could promise you more, or different,
But this is just a momentary glimpse
Of a time to which we've sealed the door.

Still, let my advice lie here.

Let knowledge linger as chocolate does
On the tongue, let it from block, melt,
Saturate; you, salivate, and let your buds
Evaluate the taste, and your reply;
Sing it, as the taste you believe should be sung.

Forget reviews, forget previews into the soul
By the paper permit with the name of a Place
As if a name is all there is to be told, and know:
You stand on the shoulders of statues who
Never knew as much as you, and never knew
That the burdens of all the miracles they made
Would fall onto the eighteen, twenty year old you.

Never was a university meant to be a factory
And never was discovery meant to be diving deep,
Mining into specializations from just past infancy,
Yet your reality is this, but I hope that at least
Through all of the mist, this drop of hope in a poem,
Might have relieved a little, your drowning, dry lips,
And I say this as one who before this, grew,
And cannot apologize enough to you.

Learn, discern, grow.
We will try to rectify our mistakes,
But you will shape the landscape
For those who will follow.

Tree Talks

In the sun where a grove of trees once
Laid their roots, we, a pair in a row,
Drank in ideas and discussions, our
Roots intertwined, and dreamed
Underneath the sun – of *Freedom*.

With the naïve bravery that is fertilized
By equal portions of bluff and love, we
Wished for crisis, as if only through
Ordeal we could prove what we were
Made of. Before long, the gusts picked up.

And now that turbulent times have
Begun to tear into the test of our ages,
Our roots have been torn apart.
Now, stripped bare to our trunks,
We've found that bark is as tough as fluff.

A CITY LIKE A STONE

A City Like a Stone

I've never seen a city plunge
Into the sea only to find
That it was a plop in a pond.

And while teardrops and rain
And the dew that drips down is
Forgotten in the grand scheme

Of a Day, when you watch
Water collide with water,
Driven by the inevitability

Of Gravity, the scattering of
What seems like little baubles
Scatters countless, smaller spheres.

So when this city sinks
Like a stone, a modern-day
Atlantis sinking eventually

Into mythology, don't forget
To watch the following burp
Of protest that emerges like

The hungry tongue of a
Hummingbird, flitting,
And that final, following

Drop that is expunged,
And then follows the city's
Destined, drowned plunge.

Pickpocket

I've seen in the movies,
"Men in Black", Galaxy
Around the cat's neck:

I should've hoped
That Hollywood wasn't
Selling me an untruth.

Pickpocket me a city.

If you could shrink
This island like "Antman"
Did a tank on a keychain:

I should have wished
That Hollywood wasn't
Selling me a story.

Pickpocket me a city.

If "Inception" and "Dr. Strange"
Could fold cities into squares
Then take these skyscrapers:

I would have puzzled it out,
If Hollywood could
Rubik's cube a lie into truth.

Pickpocket me a city.

Dimensions

You, who accuse us of
idiocy, idleness, ignorance –
let me lay upon you some wisdom
at length, and praise you
at least for getting the
first letter right; I, you
narcissistic bastards, I, I,
I, spinning around

chasing
your own
tales till
you bore
a hole into
the ground,
I, i, no longer
capital, but
demoted to
the dot, one
dimension
of thought.

Because what you have not is the arms
to move beyond self-centeredness,
nor the depth of heart for empathy,
too cold to know the heart is as wide as the seas,
replacing that with brittle sheets of transparency
one wrong step with you, ice-cold treachery.

And most importantly, you lack the ability
to consider one dimension more – from the
pits of your beings – that the core of existence is more than
just an I for pleasant sights, more than a mine,
digging up life as your present – you still, fossil
stones, blind, unable to comprehend at all that:

The young are learning and leaning out from the
darkness of the past, fighting fate to change the
direction of present ways, reversing dusk to dawn,
buying time with desperation, possessing what you
have not, wisdom of all the damn dimensions.

Street Food

Though they sit, seeming listless,
Some with dead eyes,
They mouth silent cries as they chew
White rice from oil-stained paper boxes
And meat and bread secretly donated.

Forty days of silence and neglect.

Tired youth hunger for a future
That no others help protect.

Apathy

Apathy sits around the crook of your neck
Like a fur scarf —
This was dead when I got it.
The crooning drones on as time tickles
The hairs out of your head, one nanometer at a time;
See, with lightning that flashes, all storms eventually pass
With cracks in the sky and booms that do not last.

Still. When one day you measure your life,
Donning a new crown of white,
I wonder if you'll wonder
What it all came down to,
And if, by then, the fur you wore
Around your neck,
Might have fossilized instead into a
Spiked, stone noose of regret.

Karaoke

When the empty padded room
Filled with the flesh of voices,
Somewhere in-between the heart
And brain, the two intertwined, so that
Out past the meandering tongue and
Out the delta of the lips,
The transferral between the screen and
The empty orchestra
Completed the emptying of the flesh,
Dumping time until
Exhaustion had hit,
And bodies collapsed,
Tumbling back to
The reality of
The weekend's end,
And the dark of night-time.

Middle-aged, occupied,
They paid the sum
Folded in black padding.
With every step, the dam of
Feeling cracked and trickled
Till, as they swept down those
Corridors, the empty rooms
Devoid of flesh and singing,
Forced realization clamoured
That though summer
Was here, and the orchestras
Were ready to be filled;

The usual summer vacation patrons
Had spent their holidays
Standing street side
With their fleshy vessels
Shouting slogans
At an empty orchestra too,
And that was what they did
This summer.

Song for The Unsung Hues of Blue

I will sing for you,
Because when it seems that the world
Has pressed all the weight of hate against you,
The body-armour you don
Must feel heavier by two tonnes,
And the pain from angry glares
With the nips of jeers and cheers
Must chafe under that armour
Alongside of the sweat of hours.

I will sing to you,
Because the stench of curse words
And the accusations of crimes
You have no personal connection with, must
Curdle in the hollow echoes of those helmets,
And because, despite how it might appear,
Standing in black garb and gear
Does not render you immune to fear.

I will sing for you,
Because the duty to protect those
Next to you must be a pledge
That stands solid, cemented
By orders handed down to you,
So even as doubts leak through,
The bonds of order, brotherhood,
Sisterhood, must ring more true.

I will sing for you,
Because not all blue is black.
Because the cyan light of day
Is not the same as the evening shade
Cascading over in an azure stain.
Because the cerulean shallows, reversed,

Are the same as the underworld
Of the deep sea, where creatures
Are unknowingly cursed, simply because they exist.
The pressure of leagues of sea
Is the pressure of nightmares,
Yet light is the searing terror
For those whose eyes have permanent shutters.

I will sing for you,
Because shades of blue
Do not make you ice,
Unable to tremble with the
Coldness of terror and rage,
Or with worries akin
To those you face.

I will sing for you.
I will sing for you.
I will sing for you,
Because this, still,
Is another part
Of my heart's song.

October 2nd, 2019

It doesn't matter how brightly the sun shines
The gloom is in the city
Where the lights glitter business as usual
While the bulbs wonder why their radiance
Doesn't reach the heads below.

Jaws chew like rotors pump
But eyes have finally given into gravity
And though the world rotates
And will continue to, as it always has done
On some days, if we could have our say
We'd like time, for a moment, to stop.

Sunday, Causeway Bay

Finally, for the first time,
As we trekked old streets
Where shopping was once galore;
We listened as sudden pops
Exploded like the beginning of
Show-time does, or sudden confetti,
With smoke that emits off
A campfire blaze, or a candle
On the top of a birthday cake,

And I was swept back to
Comparisons with playground play,
When we made juiceboxes swell
Jumping on them to make great bangs;
When we folded paper in certain ways,
Just four times, chopping it down
Like a machete to make a great crack:
When we had pop-candy which sizzled
Atop of tongues and the pops in our
Mouths were little rewards of sugar:

Uncomprehending, we stood, then
Walked away from the bangs
That emerged from the streets. We
Marched one-two, one-two, away
From the smoke that rose up, up,
Caught in the crowd (playing no
Playground games, for the cops
And robbers seemed one and the same),
We marched, as new clouds
On old streets made eyes cry,
And old memories and new writhed
In this city's new Sunday sights.

The gas that rose after those
Cracking crescendos reminded us
Of playground bullies playing
Their own game, and of teachers,
Outside of the mist, who smiled,
Taking their side, stating that,
In their eyes, they
Had applied "utmost restraint".

Liberty

What does a future look like?
It has a colour.
White, black, red, a landscape,
Whatever you're pleased by,
Because your mind's eye
Is a mouse;
IMAGINATION, the program you run it on;
And as it runs wild,
The mouse is a flickering paintbrush
That dances on tools and colours and gradients
And shades and flails because
The one holding it is you,
A cat trying to catch the mouse drawing the future
In your imagination.

But one thing futures don't look like
Is a landscape
That doesn't change;
Copy, paste, copy, paste,
A template that
doesn't alter
In shape, size,
Or colour.

So how do you make a future?
You begin just as a point,
In the vision you wish to create.
You stand, and resist as wave after wave
Bashes against you and those who feel the same.
After the paint dries, those who remain standing,
Determine the future's shape.

Advance Comment

These poems are a love letter to Hong Kong, and a tribute to the small joys that the city offers those who slow down and take stock of their surroundings. The collection takes us on a spatial and temporal journey through the city, offering solace and familiarity in a time of change. It is often so difficult to write about Hong Kong without resorting to orientalist and colonial tropes, and Jon has quietly defied these stereotypes with nuanced lines that brim with honesty and emotion. Jon Ng is not only a Hong Kong poet but a true Hong Konger in every sense of the word.

—Karen Cheung, editor and journalist, Hong Kong

SOME POETRY AND POETRY COLLECTIONS
Published by Proverse Hong Kong

Alphabet, by Andrew S. Guthrie. 2015.

Astra and Sebastian, by L.W. Illsley. 2011.

Bliss of Bewilderment, by Birgit Bunzel Linder. 2017.

The Burning Lake, by Jonathan Locke Hart. 2016.

Celestial Promise, by Hayley Ann Solomon. 2017.

Chasing light, by Patricia Glinton Meicholas. 2013.

China suite and other poems,
by Gillian Bickley. 2009.

Epochal Reckonings, by J.P. Linstroth, 2020. *(Scheduled.)*

For the record and other poems of Hong Kong,
by Gillian Bickley. 2003.

Frida Kahlo's cry and other poems,
by Laura Solomon. 2015.

Grandfather's Robin, by Gillian Bickley, 2020.

Heart to Heart: Poems, by Patty Ho. 2010.

Home, away, elsewhere,
by Vaughan Rapatahana. 2011.

Hong Kong Growing Pains, by Jon Ng. 2020.

Immortelle and bhandaaraa poems,
by Lelawattee Manoo-Rahming. 2011.

In vitro, by Laura Solomon. 2nd ed. 2014.

Irreverent poems for pretentious people,
by Henrik Hoeg. 2016.

The layers between (essays and poems),
by Celia Claase. 2015.

Of leaves & ashes, by Patty Ho. 2016.

Life Lines, by Shahilla Shariff. 2011.

Mingled voices: the international Proverse Poetry Prize anthology 2016,
edited by Gillian and Verner Bickley. 2017.

Mingled voices 2: the international Proverse Poetry Prize anthology 2017,
edited by Gillian and Verner Bickley. 2018.

Mingled voices 3: the international Proverse Poetry Prize anthology 2018,
edited by Gillian and Verner Bickley. 2019.

Mingled voices 4: the international Proverse Poetry Prize anthology 2019,
edited by Gillian and Verner Bickley. 2020.

Moving house and other poems from Hong Kong,
by Gillian Bickley. 2005.

Over the Years: Selected Collected Poems, 1972-2015,
by Gillian Bickley. 2017.

Painting the borrowed house: poems,
by Kate Rogers. 2008.

Perceptions, by Gillian Bickley. 2012.

Poems from the Wilderness,
by Jack Mayer, 2020. (*Scheduled.*)

Rain on the pacific coast,
by Elbert Siu Ping Lee. 2013.

refrain, by Jason S. Polley. 2010.

Savage Charm, by Ahmed Elbeshlawy. 2019.

Shadow play, by James Norcliffe. 2012.

Shadows in deferment, by Birgit Bunzel Linder. 2013.

Shifting sands, by Deepa Vanjani. 2016.

Sightings: a collection of poetry, with an essay, 'communicating poems',
by Gillian Bickley. 2007.

Smoked pearl: poems of Hong Kong and beyond,
by Akin Jeje (Akinsola Olufemi Jeje). 2010.

Of symbols misused, by Mary-Jane Newton. 2011.

The Hummingbird Sometimes Flies Backwards, by D.J. Hamilton. 2019.

The Year of the Apparitions, by José Manuel Sevilla. 2020.

Unlocking, by Mary-Jane Newton. March 2014.

Violet, by Carolina Ilica. March 2019.

Wonder, lust & itchy feet, by Sally Dellow. 2011.

FIND OUT MORE ABOUT PROVERSE AUTHORS, BOOKS, EVENTS AND LITERARY PRIZES

Visit our website: http://www.proversepublishing.com
Visit our distributor's website: www.cup.cuhk.edu.hk

Follow us on Twitter
Follow news and conversation: twitter.com/Proversebooks
OR
Copy and paste the following to your browser window and follow the instructions: https://twitter.com/#!/ProverseBooks
"Like" us on www.facebook.com/ProversePress

Request our free E-Newsletter
Send your request to info@proversepublishing.com.

Availability
Available in Hong Kong and world-wide from our Hong Kong based distributor, The Chinese University of Hong Kong Press, The Chinese University of Hong Kong, Shatin, NT, Hong Kong SAR, China.
Email: cup@cuhk.edu.hk
Website: www.cup.cuhk.edu.hk.

All titles are available from Proverse Hong Kong, http://www.proversepublishing.com

Most titles can be ordered online from amazon (various countries).

Stock-holding retailers
Hong Kong (CUHKP, Bookazine)
Canada (Elizabeth Campbell Books),
Andorra (Llibreria La Puça, La Llibreria).

Orders may be made from bookshops in the UK and elsewhere.

Ebooks
Most Proverse titles are available also as Ebooks.

www.ingramcontent.com/pod-product-compliance
Lightning Source LLC
Chambersburg PA
CBHW061258140726
47998CB00006B/2272